The *Pathfinder* Series

Active learning — listening and reading

Creative use of texts (PF21)
Bernard Kavanagh & Lynne Upton .... ISBN 1 874016 28 3

Listening in a foreign language (PF26)
A skill we take for granted?
Karen Turner .... ISBN 1 874016 44 5

Stimulating grammatical awareness (PF33)
A fresh look at language acquisition
Heather Rendall .... ISBN 1 902031 08 3

More reading for pleasure in a foreign language (PF36)
Ann Swarbrick .... ISBN 1 902031 13 X

Supporting learners and learning

Teaching learners how to learn
Strategy training in the ML classroom (PF31)
Vee Harris .... ISBN 1 874016 83 6

Making effective use of the dictionary (PF28)
Gwen Berwick and Phil Horsfall .... ISBN 1 874016 60 7

Nightshift (PF20)
Ideas and strategies for homework
David Buckland & Mike Short .... ISBN 1 874016 19 4

Grammar matters (PF17)
Susan Halliwell .... ISBN 1 874016 12 7

On course for GCSE coursework (PF35)
Julie Adams .... ISBN 1 902031 26 1

Pairwork (PF38)
Interaction in the modern languages classroom
Wendy Phipps .... ISBN 1 902031 28 8

Planning and organising teaching

Assessment and planning in the MFL department (PF29)
Harmer Parr .... ISBN 1 874016 71 2

Getting the best results at GCSE (PF39)
Mike Buckby & Kate Corney .... ISBN 1 902031 27 X

Foreign Language Assistants (PF32)
A guide to good practice
David Rowles, Marian Carty
& Anneli McLachlan .... ISBN 1 874016 95 X

Improve your image (PF15)
The effective use of the OHP
Daniel Tierney & Fay Humphreys .... ISBN 1 874016 04 6

Teaching/learning in the target language

On target (PF5)
Teaching in the target language
Susan Halliwell & Barry Jones .... ISBN 0 948003 54 5

Keeping on target (PF23)
Bernardette Holmes .... ISBN 1 874016 35 5

Words (PF34)
Teaching and learning vocabulary
David Snow .... ISBN 1 902031 14 8

Motivating all learners

Yes — but will they behave? (PF4)
Managing the interactive classroom
Susan Halliwell .... ISBN 0 948003 44 8

Differentiation and individual learners (PF37)
Anne Convery & Do Coyle .... ISBN 1 902031 10 5

Cultural awareness

Crossing frontiers (PF30)
The school study visit abroad
David Snow & Michael Byram .... ISBN 1 874016 84 4

Exploring otherness (PF24)
An approach to cultural awareness
Barry Jones .... ISBN 1 874016 42 9

Broadening the learning experience

New contexts for modern language learning (PF27)
Cross-curricular approaches
Kim Brown & Margot Brown .... ISBN 1 874016 50 X

With a song in my scheme of work (PF25)
Steven Fawkes .... ISBN 1 874016 45 3

Drama in the languages classroom (PF19)
Judith Hamilton & Anne McLeod .... ISBN 1 874016 07 0

The RESOURCE *file* Series

Changing places (RF1)
Cross-curricular approaches to teaching languages
Kim Brown & Margot Brown .... ISBN 1 902031 05 9

Getting the basics right (RF3)
Nouns, gender and adjectives
Lydia Biriotti .... ISBN 1 902031 40 7

Mixed ability teaching in language learning (RF4)
Susan Ainslie & Sue Purcell .... ISBN 1 902031 53 9

CILT Publications are available through good book suppliers or direct from
Central Books, 99 Wallis Rd, London E9 5LN. Tel: 020 8986 4854. Fax: 020 8533 5821.
Fax orders to: 020 7379 5082. Credit card orders: 020 7379 5101 ext. 248.

RESOURCE *file 2*

Pathfinder support materials
for language teachers

Up, up and away!

Using classroom target language to help
learners say what they want to say

Tony Elston

cilt
Centre for Information
on Language Teaching and Research

This ResourceFile is dedicated, without permission, to all those pupils who have ever asked the question 'Why do we have to talk French?'.

Acknowledgements

I would like to thank Pat McLagan and James Burch for their many insights into languages teaching; Kate McEnroe and Annie Beury for drawing the original posters; the French department of Stretford High School, Manchester and the modern languages department of St Bonaventure's School, London, for their unstinting support; S Page, for teaching me Hofstadter's Law, which is the original version of Sod's law of display; and the many pupils I have taught who have tried to use classroom target language.

Finally, a special thank you to Lesley, Holly, Caitlin and Natasha, both for putting up with me and for making me look forward to getting home each day.

The author and publisher would also like to thank Oxford University Press for permission to reproduce copyright materials from parts 1, 2 and 3 of the Key Stage 3 French course, *Génial*.

First published in 2000
by the Centre for Information on Language Teaching and Research (CILT)
20 Bedfordbury
London
WC2N 4LB

Copyright © 2000 Centre for Information on Language Teaching and Research

Illustrations by Kate Taylor

ISBN 1 902031 25 3

1002081446

A catalogue record for this book is available from the British Library

Printed in Great Britain by The Cromwell Press

Contents

Introduction   1

1 Where we are now, and how to move on   3

**2 Teaching learner classroom target language –
using the classroom target language posters**   8

3 Consolidation and reinforcement   13

4 Extending pupils' target language   20

5 Creating your own departmental posters   28

6 Developing your department's target language policy   35

Photocopiable materials

Section 2

Classroom language posters   39

Section 3

Feuilles d'étudiant   84

Feuilles de consolidation   87

Further reading   90

Photocopiable pages

Introduction

As part of the making of the CILT/St Martin's College video resource, *Opening the door on the modern languages classroom*, my work with a challenging Year 9 French class was recorded over the course of a year. In my own case, the focus of filming was on promoting and sustaining pupil target language.

Watching and discussing recordings of my lessons helped me evaluate my practice, and by the end of the project I realised what is now widely agreed:

'It is [also] important to create a supportive environment, which includes not only physical aspects, such as wall displays, but also a psychological environment which encourages pupils to "have a go".'

Target practice: developing pupils' use of the target language (National Curriculum Council)

It was clear to me that getting right the 'physical aspects' of support would give a tremendous boost to developing a successful 'psychological environment'. There were, however, two major obstacles:

■ I can't draw to save my life, so artwork on wall displays was a problem;

■ like all teachers, I never seem to have enough time for new initiatives.

Several years on, and the excellent work of two departments later, I have had the privilege of helping develop and use a system for promoting pupil target language which provides learners with:

■ 'physical support', in the form of photocopiable classroom language posters;

■ 'psychological support', in the form of the accompanying methodology;

■ constant opportunities to *extend* their target language through careful use of the posters and methodology.

This ResourceFile brings together these tried and tested means of providing both 'physical support' and 'psychological support' and is designed to help teachers of French to:

■ create a suitable physical environment for pupil target language development;

■ develop a suitable psychological environment for pupil target language development;

■ use these physical and psychological environments to develop and *extend* pupils' target language proficiency.

And it doesn't matter if you can't draw.

Problem solving

… or lessons learned from my involvement in the CILT/St Martin's College video resource, *Opening the door on the modern languages classroom.*

My low-achieving Year 9 pupils needed to be able to refer to key classroom expressions quickly. We purchased a commercially available set but unfortunately found they were of limited value as:

- there were very few posters in the set;

- they were small and hard to read;

- most contained a lot of text;

- while the text was linguistically very correct (*Comment dit-on en français …?*), relatively little of it was easily transferable to other contexts;

- there was no obvious language progression evident in the choice of posters;

- we had no numbering system for the posters, so while I waved frantically at the display whenever one of the featured expressions was needed, by the time a pupil had actually hit on the right one, the rest of the class had forgotten the meaning we were trying to convey.

Solutions in this ResourceFile

The photocopiable classroom target language posters combine an illustration and text to produce an A3 poster (or A2 if each page is enlarged to A3):

- the text has been carefully chosen to be both visible and manageable;

- where a message can be communicated in several ways, I have opted for the way which is both easiest to remember **and** most easily transferable to other contexts, so that instead of *Comment dit-on en français …?* we have *Qu'est-ce que c'est en français …?* (The latter can be used to reinforce *Qu'est-ce que*, *c'est* and *ce que* whenever they come up in other contexts);

- the photocopiable posters support and reinforce progression by introducing classroom expressions in a carefully structured way;

- there is a suggested numbering system.

Target language and the National Curriculum

The National Curriculum Council's early monitoring of the implementation of modern foreign languages in Year 7 showed that while many **teachers** were already conducting a large part of their lessons in the target language, they had less confidence in **pupils'** ability to use and sustain the target language themselves. Today, OFSTED modern foreign language inspectors confirm that most of us still have a long way to go in getting **pupils** to use and sustain the target language in the classroom. The most important point is that pupil target language use does not happen by accident:

'The more pupils are exposed to the target language in a systematic and structured way, the more they are likely to absorb. In the long run, this will have a positive effect on pupils' language development and enjoyment in learning and using the language.'

National Curriculum Council, *Modern Foreign Languages non-statutory guidance*

This ResourceFile combines photocopiable materials with teaching strategies. Together, these offer a system of exposing pupils to French in a systematic and structured way to help them communicate more extensively. In the departments which have developed this system, it has worked by:

- highlighting key vocabulary and grammatical structures;

- showing learners how to use and personalise the above;

- offering opportunities for the practice, reinforcement and recycling of key language;

- developing learners' confidence in manipulating language in different contexts;

- suggesting ways forward for departments.

Chapter 1

Where we are now, and how to move on

Many factors determine the extent to which we, as teachers, maintain the target language studied as the 'normal language of the classroom'. These factors include:

- our own proficiency in the target language studied;
- our expectations of learners;
- the motivation of learners;
- whether there is an inspector in the room!

We know that **teacher** use of target language in the classroom is widespread. The difficulty we most frequently face is in promoting sustained **learner** target language communication. The most common reasons given by languages teachers for not pushing harder to promote learner target language communication are worries about:

- learner understanding;
- 'falling behind with the work';
- discipline problems.

These issues will be examined once we have asked a question which is especially pressing during those moments when we are at the end of our tether trying to get our most difficult class to do any work at all in **any** language …

Why encourage learners to use the target language at all?

We need to be absolutely convinced of the importance of learner target language use (even last lesson on a Friday afternoon with a difficult class!), otherwise our encouragement to pupils to play their part rings hollow. Many of the reasons given by the MFL Working Group in its final report (*Modern Foreign Languages for Ages 11 to 16*, DES/WO/HMSO, October 1990) for teaching an MFL apply equally to promoting and sustaining pupil target language:

- to develop the ability to use the language effectively for purposes of practical communication;
- to form a sound base of the skills [and] language … required for further study, work and leisure;
- to develop an awareness of the nature of language and language learning;
- to provide enjoyment and intellectual stimulation;
- to promote learning skills of more general application (e.g. analysis, memorising, drawing of inferences).

In addition:

> 'Exposure to the target language also helps learners develop a sensitivity to pronunciation, intonation, structure and meaning. This supports pupils' language acquisition without overt teaching.'
>
> *MFL non-statutory guidance*

What do you mean, you're still not absolutely convinced?

Making the language studied the normal means of communication reinforces its purpose as a means of communication and so allows for the practice, consolidation and reinforcement of language, which are all essential to successful language learning.

The ultimate aim of language teaching must be to enable learners to manipulate language to suit their own needs. Classroom communication affords learners regular opportunities to develop their manipulative skills.

The importance of this last point is demonstrated by the experience of many of our learners during trips to countries where the language is studied. They are frequently able to communicate effectively in pre-rehearsed role-play situations such as ordering a meal or seeking directions. However, far fewer are able to deal with unexpected responses which stray from pre-learned language; and fewer still are able to engage in spontaneous conversation with a native speaker.

Making the target language the 'normal language of the classroom' familiarises learners each lesson with the situation described above, and helps them to deal with it. By encouraging learners regularly to deal with unexpected language from ourselves or from fellow learners, and by equipping learners with the language and strategies they need to respond, we are helping them become independent in their language use.

You're coming round (again), but how are you supposed to convince the kids?

> A very high proportion of the vocabulary and structures needed for languages qualifications at age 16 arises naturally in everyday classroom communication.

You can get pupils to see for themselves, by showing them past examination papers such as role-play cards and writing exam questions. (You can **really** bring the point home by cheating a little, and carefully selecting those past papers whose tasks contain the highest percentage of language from the posters!).

Cases in point

They need to say 'What is a *croque-madame*?'. They simply take *Qu'est-ce que c'est en français?* from the relevant poster (photocopiable page 45) and substitute *en français* with *croque-madame*, to get '*Qu'est-ce que c'est, "un croque-madame?"* '

They need to say 'I was ill'. They take '*J'étais avec Monsieur ...*' from the relevant poster (photocopiable page 55), and substitute *avec Monsieur ...* with *malade*, to get '*J'étais malade*'.

'Yes, but ...'

'Yes, but they won't understand.'

'Yes, but we'll fall behind with the work.'

'Yes, but they won't behave for long enough.'

These concerns prevent many teachers attempting to promote learner target language with some classes. *Up, up and away!* offers strategies to reduce the effect of these hurdles, but it is worth making a few points now.

'Yes, but they won't understand'

Everything is teachable. That's the easy bit. The hard bit is that the challenge (and it is a challenge which exercises the minds of most teachers until retirement!) is to break everything up into small enough parts to help individual learners progress from one stage to the next. *Up, up and away!* offers strategies for promoting learner target language use in a structured way.

Barry Jones of Homerton College, Cambridge, was asked at a conference what real chance learners with special educational needs had of coping in languages lessons conducted entirely in the target language. He replied by asking what chance they had if lessons were *not* conducted in the target language.

'Yes, but we'll fall behind with the work'

Research conducted by James Burch at St Martin's College, Lancaster, has consistently proved two things. A class whose teacher has adopted a fresh and sustained approach to promoting learner use of the target language typically covers less of a textbook-based syllabus than a class of parallel ability in the first one or two terms.

However, the class which has been actively encouraged to use and manipulate target language at every opportunity has a far stronger grasp of structures than their peers in the other class. This enables them to make far faster progress by the third term, and they soon 'overtake' the other class before steaming ahead.

'Yes, but they won't behave for long enough'

My own work with learners of all abilities has shown me that it is possible for all groups to increase significantly their use of the target language for classroom communication. *Up, up and away!* includes strategies to help reluctant learners progress. Many of these strategies were learned the hard way, with a challenging third set of Year 9 boys. My work with them features on the video *Opening the door on the modern languages classroom* (see bibliography).

Language-learning aims

Recent OFSTED reports have highlighted the need for language teachers to focus more on the National Curriculum Programme of Study Part 1 in their planning of lessons. Parts 1 and 2 are replaced in the Revised National Curriculum by two sorts of requirements: knowledge, skills and understanding; and breadth of study. We have made these requirements a focus of our planning. The table on page 7 gives an overview of those learning opportunities identified in these two sorts of requirements which are central to the approach of this ResourceFile.

Expecting the unexpected

In my first year of teaching, one of my classes was a challenging mixed ability Year 7 group. I was enormously surprised when one pupil asked, '*Je peux avoir un crayon?*'. Although I had taught the class the expression and had told them I wanted them to speak French wherever possible, I had taken no steps to encourage them to use the target language. In other words, my actions, or rather my lack of them, belied my words. Despite this, the pupil had taken my words at face value, which is why I can still remember his name!

Unfortunately, though I praised him at the time, I failed to build on his good work by not raising my expectations of the class's ability to use classroom target language. In short, as with all aspects of education, our expectations are crucial to learners' success. Our challenge is to ensure that our expectations of learners' classroom target language use are at once high and achievable. The chapters which follow are intended to help us help learners help themselves.

up, up and away!

Revised National Curriculum Programme of Study				
Knowledge, skills and understanding				**Breadth of Study**
Acquiring knowledge and understanding of the target language	**Developing language skills**	**Developing language-learning skills**		*5 During Key Stages 3 and 4, pupils should be taught the Knowledge, skills and understanding through:*
1 Pupils should be taught:	*2 Pupils should be taught:*	*3 Pupils should be taught:*		
a the principles and inter-relationship of sounds and writing in the target language	b correct pronunciation and intonation	a techniques for memorising words, phrases and short extracts		a communicating in the target language in pairs and groups, and with their teacher
b the grammar of the target language and how to apply it	c how to ask and answer questions	b how to use context and other clues to interpret meaning		b using everyday classroom events as an opportunity for spontaneous speech
c how to express themselves using a range of vocabulary and structures	e how to vary the target language to suit context, audience and purpose	c to use their knowledge of English or another language when learning the target language		c expressing and discussing personal feelings and opinions
	f how to adapt language they already know for different contexts	e how to develop their independence in learning and using the target language		
	g strategies for dealing with the unpredictable			

Chapter 2

Teaching learner classroom target language –
using the classroom target language posters

What's in it for me? ... or the pupil question we must address to succeed

To win over pupils whose immediate instinct is **not** to be won over, we must:

■ explain why we're pushing them to use the target language (please see page 3);

■ encourage the target language through verbal rewards ('*Bravo!*') as well as tangible rewards (merits, stars in homework diary, comments to parents, form teachers, stickers and so on);

■ keep going!

Using the classroom target language posters

Pages 40 to 82 consist of photocopiable double pages, with each double page making a poster featuring a classroom expression below a picture which illustrates the expression.

The double pages are sequenced in a suggested order of introduction. The sequence is based primarily on past classroom practice showing the likely frequency with which learners will want to use a particular expression.

If you are able to put copies of the posters up on your classroom wall, first decide on which posters to use. Your choice could be determined by;

■ which groups you are targetting most;

■ classroom language you wish to reinforce with those groups;

■ new classroom language you wish those groups to use.

You will need to decide whether to put up posters after you have taught the language orally, or before. Whilst some teachers are wary of pupils seeing an expression before they know how to pronounce it, in practice the need for a particular expression can arise at any time. Not having a poster up can mean a missed opportunity to reinforce the language visually. An effective compromise is to display a sequence of posters but draw the class's attention to how an expression is written only when you have taught the expression orally.

If you are not able to display posters on a classroom wall, perhaps because you teach in a variety of non-specialist rooms, having this ResourceFile with you in lessons enables you to show any expression and the accompanying illustration needed by a class. You can do this more quickly by adding Post-its to the edges of the pages you use most often. Post-its in different colours enable you to locate quickly pages more appropriate to different groups.

Numbering the posters

Apart from page numbers in small script for your reference, the posters are not numbered. This allows total flexibility as regards the order in which you introduce the classroom expressions. However, to refer learners to a particular poster quickly, you need to number each poster. A numbered Post-it on each poster works well.

Teaching with the posters (photocopiable pages 44 to 49)

The 'asking for help' posters *Je peux parler en anglais?*
and *Qu'est-ce que c'est en français …?*

Although it is important that learners use these two expressions sparingly, they are especially useful early on. Stress to the class that these two expressions are essential, and teach them as you would any new word or phrase accompanied by a flashcard.

Je peux parler en anglais?

When learners wish to convey an idea they cannot express in French, they can seek permission by asking, '*Je peux parler en anglais?*'. You can reinforce the importance of French as the language of the classroom by asking the class, '*Je peux parler en anglais?*' if you need to go into

English yourself. Once a learner has said what they need to say in English, you can either:

■ leave it at that, if putting it into French would be too involved;

■ teach or revise the appropriate French classroom expression, if on the wall;

  or

■ teach a simple way of getting the message across, using an expression on the wall.

Some teachers operate a 'safe area', to which pupils can go if they feel they must say something they cannot say in the target language. Pupils must, of course, request permission in the target language to go to the safe area.

How not to do it

Once, when a pupil was late for my lesson, I stopped the lesson to try and teach the class the French for 'Sorry I am late. I was handing in the dinner money'. Fifteen minutes later, the class, who found French hard anyway, were none the wiser for their botched repetition of my drawn out translation.

Today I would focus on the most important parts of the message and see how they could be adapted to relate to other situations. Thus with a class who had never before said *'Excusez-moi, je suis en retard'* (photocopiable pages 41 and 52–53), I would focus on that alone. As for a class who already knew how to apologise in French, I would get them to extend their apology by adding an easily transferable expression:

'Excusez-moi, je suis en retard. J'étais avec Madame [name of person in the office to whom dinner money is given]' (photocopiable pages 41 and 54–55).

These can be seen in the table below.

Expected target language to convey: 'Sorry I am late. I was handing in the dinner money.'		
More support	**Less support**	**Least support**
Excusez-moi, (p 41) je suis en retard. (pp 52–53)	Excusez-moi, (p 41) je suis en retard. J'étais avec Madame [*name of person*] (pp 54–55).	Finally, I would get a very able class to translate the full expression themselves, giving any appropriate help: T: En français *'to give back'*, c'est 'rendre'. '*I was giving back*', c'est l'imparfait ou le passé composé? L: L'imparfait. T: Bravo! Alors qu'est-ce que c'est en français, '*I was giving back*'? L: Je rendais. T: Très bien. Et en français, *'pocket money'* c'est *'l'argent de poche'*. Alors qu'est-ce que c'est 'dinner money' pensez-vous? L: L'argent de déjeuner. T: Bravo.

Qu'est-ce que c'est en français ...?

Learners can use this to seek:

■ a whole phrase from you or from a fellow pupil;

■ a word to complete a phrase they already know.

In this example, the learner wishes to ask for a tissue and knows *Je peux avoir ...?* (photocopiable pages 50–51).

L: *Qu'est-ce que c'est en français,* 'a tissue'?

T: *Un Kleenex.*

L: *Je peux avoir un Kleenex?*

T: *Bravo! Voici un Kleenex.*

Tips on copying and displaying the posters are given on page 17.

Teaching a new classroom language expression

You can think of the classroom language posters as flashcards and introduce each as you would flashcard vocabulary, with the text covered whilst pupils are learning the correct pronounciation. As with flashcards, you can use three-stage questioning to reinforce the correct expression until the class can produce the correct expression unaided.

Each stage involves you pointing to the appropriate poster. In the example below, the class needs to be able to say 'I have forgotten my exercise book.'

Stage 1
T: *Oui ou non? J'ai oublié mon cahier.*
C: *Oui.*
T: *Bravo!*

Stage 2
T: *'J'ai oublié mon cahier' ou 'J'ai oublié mon stylo'?*
C: *J'ai oublié mon cahier.*
T: *Bravo!*

Stage 3
T: *Qu'est-ce que c'est en français?*
C: *J'ai oublié mon cahier.*
T: *Bravo!*

Obviously some learners will need all three stages of questioning, whilst others can start at Stage 2, or if they are very confident, dispense completely with Stages 1 and 2. With this example, you can further stretch able learners by offering a choice of very close alternatives: '*Qu'est-ce que c'est en français? "Je n'ai pas de cahier" ou "J'ai oublié mon cahier"?*' However, as a rule it is best to avoid trying to 'catch out' pupils since this can confuse rather than teach. The most important thing when staging questions to teach new language is to build learners' confidence by helping them get the right answers whilst decreasing the support you offer as soon as they are ready.

Revising a previously encountered classroom language expression

When learners need a classroom expression already encountered, decide how much support they need to find it on the wall. For example, a learner wishes to say 'I do not have a book' (photocopiable pages 58–59). We will assume this poster is Number 7 on your wall.

Je n'ai pas de | **livre.**
stylo.
partenaire.

Getting a pupil to say 'I do not have a book.'		
More support	**Less support**	**Least support**
T: [pointing to the correct poster] Regarde le numéro sept. '*I do not have a book*', c'est 'Je n'ai pas de livre'. Répète: 'Je n'ai pas …' L: Je n'ai pas … T: de livre. L: de livre. T: Je n'ai pas de livre. L: Je n'ai pas de livre. T: Bravo!	T: [pointing to the row of posters] '*I do not have a book*', c'est le numéro sept ou le numéro huit? L: Sept. T: Bravo. C'est 'Je n'ai pas de partenaire' ou 'Je n'ai pas de livre'? L: Je n'ai pas de livre. T: Bravo!	T: [pointing to the row of posters] '*I do not have a book*', c'est quel numéro? L: Sept. T: Bravo. Alors, qu'est-ce que c'est en français '*I do not have a book*'? L: Je n'ai pas de livre. T: Bravo!

Further tips on copying and displaying the posters are given on page 17.

Chapter **3**

Consolidation and reinforcement

Using the pupil reference sheets (*Feuilles d'étudiant* – photocopiable pages 84 to 86)

These are designed for easy pupil reference and self-testing.

Self-testing understanding of the expressions

By covering the illustrations, learners can see whether they understand the meaning of each expression. To check, they uncover the matching illustration.

Self-testing by pupils of their ability to produce the expressions

By covering the expressions, pupils can see whether they can produce the expression for each illustration, either orally or in writing.

You can, of course, create your own pupil checklist by cutting and pasting any illustrations and text from a photocopy of these original ResourceFile pages. This may be useful if you have taught expressions in a different order to that on the original pages.

You can further exploit the pupil checklists by cutting the illustrations from a copy of a pupil's reference sheet and separating the illustrations from each other: pupils match the correct illustration to each expression. If you use the overhead projector, pupils can come up individually. Alternatively, by copying and cutting up enough sets, pupils could do this matching activity in pairs or individually.

Listening

Pupils write down numbers 1–10 if you are going to ask them 10 questions in the assessment. On the overhead projector, label ten illustrations from **a** to **j**. Call out the French for one of the expressions illustrated. Beside question 1 pupils write the *letter* of the matching illustration. Imagine that the illustration for question 1 is letter **d**.

T: (1) *Je suis en retard.*

(Pupils write down **d** for number 1)

Reading

Cut the illustrations side from a copy of a pupil's checklist and stick this onto the left-hand side of a blank piece of paper. At the foot of the page or on a separate piece of paper, set out a copy of each expression in random order. Pupils find the correct expression for each illustration.

Orally

You can assess pupils individually in a separate assessment or at the beginning or end of a normal individual oral assessment. Cover up the text and ask each pupil to say it by looking only at the illustrations.

In writing

Cut the illustrations side from a copy of a pupil checklist and stick this onto the left-hand side of a blank piece of paper. Pupils write the correct French to the right of each illustration.

Photocopiable reinforcement activity worksheets for pupil use (*Feuilles de consolidation* pages 87 to 89)

Pupils complete these in class or for homework. The expressions on each sheet follow the order of the posters in this ResourceFile. If you introduce the language on the posters in a different order, you may have to help learners with some of the answers.

Answers to 87

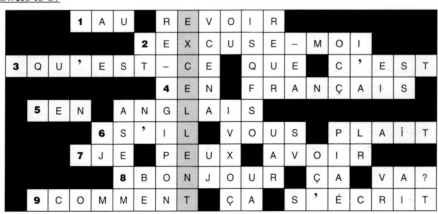

Answers to 88

		1			2								3			
8 ▶	J	E	P	E	U	X	A	V	O	I	R	...	?	P		
		S			B									A		
9 ▶	J	'	É	T	A	I	S	A	V	E	C			R		
					E									T		
10 ▶	J	E	N	'	A	I	P	A	S	D	E			N		
					T									A		

11 ▶ O N C O P I E Ç A ?   12 ▶ C A H I E R

       4▼   5▼   6▼

13 ▶ C ' E S T Q U E L L E P A G E ?

14 ▶ F E U I L L E   7▼

15 ▶ J ' A I O U B L I É

Answers to 89

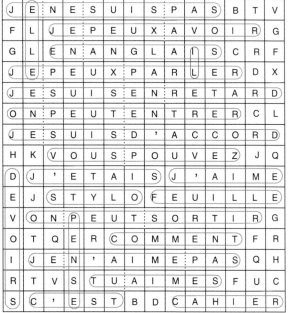

J	E	N	E	S	U	I	S	P	A	S	B	T	V
F	L	J	E	P	E	U	X	A	V	O	I	R	G
G	L	E	N	A	N	G	L	A	I	S	C	R	F
J	E	P	E	U	X	P	A	R	L	E	R	D	X
J	E	S	U	I	S	E	N	R	E	T	A	R	D
O	N	P	E	U	T	E	N	T	R	E	R	C	L
J	E	S	U	I	S	D	'	A	C	C	O	R	D
H	K	V	O	U	S	P	O	U	V	E	Z	J	Q
D	J	'	E	T	A	I	S	J	'	A	I	M	E
E	J	S	T	Y	L	O	F	E	U	I	L	L	E
V	O	N	P	E	U	T	S	O	R	T	I	R	G
O	T	Q	E	R	C	O	M	M	E	N	T	F	R
I	J	E	N	'	A	I	M	E	P	A	S	Q	H
R	T	V	S	T	U	A	I	M	E	S	F	U	C
S	C	'	E	S	T	B	D	C	A	H	I	E	R

What? When? How?

Deciding on what classroom language expressions to introduce, when to introduce them, and how

This will always be determined by the classroom language which learners are already able to produce. You need to ensure that the posters on display cater for the whole ability range. Very weak learners may take a considerable time to produce consistently correctly *s'il vous plaît* and *merci*. Unless you can refer such learners to these posters when they need help, they will take even longer to master these expressions.

Very able learners with plenty of French behind them will be able relatively quickly to produce from memory all the language on the posters. The next stage will be to put up new, extended expressions which they need next. These learners are unlikely to need the same degree of support they have had until now in their courses. It should therefore be perfectly feasible to display the text only of key expressions. You could help very able learners extend their range of classroom language by:

- each week putting up a new *expression de la semaine*;

- listing a range of responses to a question ('*Pourquoi es-tu en retard?*' '*J'ai raté le bus/Je n'ai pas entendu le réveil/Mon chien a vomi …*');

- inviting pupils to extend a particular response each lesson or week: '*J'ai oublié mon cahier …* [week 2:] *parce que j'ai oublié de consulter mon emploi du temps …* [week 3] *comme j'étais très fatigué/fatiguée …* [week 4:] *après avoir regardé la télé jusqu'à quatre heures du matin …* [week 5:] *à cause d'un film passionnant sur …*;

- getting the class to use dictionaries (and refer to verb tables if necessary) to construct new expressions as the need for these arises.

Your choice of which posters to display first will depend on the classroom language which learners are already able to produce

How you might start off your wall for beginners:

1

2

3

4

5

6

How you might start off your wall for intermediate learners who have no difficulty producing the language on the posters on pages 40–65:

1

2

3

4

5

6

7

8

9

10

Departmental policy

Just as all department members follow a common syllabus, so your learners will derive maximum benefit if you agree a department choice of posters to be added to periodically. You can then ensure that all learners in a year group will be able to understand and produce the same range of core expressions.

Please see Chapter 6 on developing a departmental target language policy.

Surprise, surprise, we need all the posters up together!

You may well decide that displaying all the posters from the start is the best way to offer all your learners the classroom language expressions they need. You may wish to divide up the posters into two or more sections. For instance, you could have a beginners' section, with the early posters; an intermediates' section with a range of posters from the middle of the series; and a section aimed at more advanced learners, with posters coming from the end of the series. Such a scheme has infinite permutations. You could, for instance, devote part of a wall to posters aimed at beginners, then move posters into this section as learners develop their use of classroom language. (This has the advantage of enabling learners to see concretely just how much progress they have made by the end of the year, by which time the beginners' section is awash with posters.) However, be very wary of ...

Sod's law of display

Sod's law of display states that putting up a display will always take considerably longer than you think, **even after you have taken into account Sod's law of display**.

Tips on copying and displaying the posters

Preparing and displaying the posters **takes time.** It is therefore essential to

- be realistic;
- be careful;
- remember Sod's law of display (please see above).

Nevertheless, if you intend the posters to be a focal point of the classroom from now on, it is worth taking the time to make a lasting display. The initial investment in time and effort is repaid many times over as pupils develop their confidence in using the classroom expressions.

In my last two departments, we spent a lot of time getting it right, but once we were happy with the display it needed only very occasional work to stay fresh. The result is that, no matter which languages classroom you enter in those schools, you are drawn to the array of colourful posters with clear text in the target language. We used rolls of backing paper (bright yellow is my favourite) along the walls to make the posters look more attractive, taking care to position the posters out of immediate reach of pupils, but where they are visible to the whole class. A good idea is to go round your school looking at displays, and borrow ideas from those you like most. If you do use backing paper, always keep some spare. This way if, for instance, some ink finds its way onto a section, you can stick a small section of your spare backing paper over the offending part instead of having to replace the whole roll.

Copying the posters

Questions to ask before you start

- Which posters shall we copy first?
- Do we make copies for the whole department?
- How many spare copies do we need?
- Would it be helpful to colour code the posters, for example with your core expressions or Year 7 expressions on one colour, Year 8 on another and so on?
- Where will we store the spare copies we do not immediately put up?
- Which posters shall we copy next time?
- When do we expect 'next time' to be?
- Where do we keep this ResourceFile?

Making copies

Check the copying toner by making a couple of trial copies: poor quality copies will be harder to read and will not look nearly as good.

Copy each single page in this ResourceFile onto A3 size paper to make A2-sized posters. This can be done either by using the automatic A4 ➔ A3 feature, or by increasing the size by 141%. Then place the A3 illustration above the A3 text poster.

If wall space is at a premium and you prefer A3-sized posters combining both an illustration and text, you may wish to make the illustration outlines bolder with a felt-tip pen. (Or reward willing pupils to do this for you!)

If you wish to avoid the spiral binding between the artwork and text, place a long, thin strip of paper over the spiral binding before copying.

You can store extra copies either folded in A4-size plastic pockets, or you can purchase A3 size plastic pockets and especially large ringbinders from most school stationery suppliers.

Once you have the copies

If you feel you could benefit from the therapeutic effects of colouring them in yourself with bold felt pens, go ahead. Otherwise, ask reliable pupils to colour them in for you.

Decide whether you are happy to leave the choice of colours to pupils, or whether you wish all the young people depicted in the posters to wear the colours of your school's uniform.

It is worth considering laminating the posters, especially if your school is fortunate enough to have an obliging media resources officer who can do this for you.

Pin up the posters, taking care to position them where they are clearly visible but preferably out of the reach of pupils who might try and damage them.

Use bold felt pens on Post-its positioned either directly above or on top of each poster to number each poster.

Avoid writing numbers onto the posters themselves, as this commits you to keeping them in the same sequence.

If you still feel adventurous and want to reinforce numbers other than those from 1–25 with your pupils, you could instead number the posters from 75–100.

Another alternative to numbering them 1–25 is to reinforce the French alphabet by writing a letter of the alphabet above each poster (once you reach Z you can use A2, B2 and so on).

Health and Safety

Your LEA or school's Health and Safety policy may well include detailed guidelines on displaying work safely in terms of, for example, the use of stepladders. Following these guidelines should help you avoid personal injury. **Failure** to follow these guidelines may result in your loss of entitlement to compensation for any industrial injury suffered as a result of displaying materials.

Similarly, you need to be extremely cautious before involving either colleagues or pupils in putting up display materials. If in doubt, consult your school's Health and Safety representative or headteacher.

Finally ...

Keep referring to, and referring learners to, the posters. This will enable you to find your way round them very quickly, and so help learners derive maximum benefit from consulting the posters themselves. You can refer to a poster:

■ to help the class locate a classroom language expression;

■ to illustrate a vocabulary or grammatical point using language from a poster.

The more you refer learners to the posters, the more quickly they:

■ find their way around them;

■ help themselves;

■ help each other.

Examinations

Public exams do not usually allow pupils to use the kind of help the posters offer. If in doubt, check with your school's examinations officer or with the appropriate Examinations Board. Clearly you can decide with your department whether to allow learners the support of the posters in internal exams.

The easiest way of 'removing' the posters is by temporarily pinning a roll of backing paper over them – preferably with a colour you are stuck with but do not want to use for display!

Chapter 4

Extending pupils' target language

Using the classroom posters as a springboard

Even beginners can memorise and use short phrases containing relatively complex structures when encouraged to treat these phrases as useful lexical items.

Almost all the posters contain language you can highlight to teach and reinforce grammatical points as they arise during the course. The list below is a guide, but is far from exhaustive. By using language from the posters with which learners are already familiar, you can develop awareness of structures more effectively since

- rules become more concrete when learners can relate them to language they have already grasped;
- learners have familiar examples of the rules in context to work with when trying to manipulate language.

Take the case of a pupil who wants to say s/he was absent on a particular day. Refer the pupil to the relevant poster (photocopiable pages 54–55): *J'étais avec Monsieur/Madame … .* Once they know that *j'étais* means 'I was', you can get them to replace *avec* with *absent* to create a new expression they want to use (especially if it is the reason why they have not done their homework).

As a more involved example, many learners who are comfortable using the *passé composé* in the affirmative have no difficulty saying in accurate French 'Last night I watched TV'. However, many of these learners find it enormously difficult to say in accurate French 'I did not watch TV last night'.

If these learners can produce from memory *'Je n'ai pas de livre'* (photocopiable pages 58–59) because they have known *'je n'ai pas de'* since the beginning of their course, they have already grasped from one context – saying they have no book – the language they need for a new context – saying they did not watch TV last night. In this example, moving learners from the first context to the second appears protracted, but it is a technique we can quickly develop once we know our way round the classroom language posters.

The flow chart below illustrates how to move a learner from a known context to an unknown one by getting learners to draw on their own knowledge. In this example, the learner's interjections have been merged with the teacher's so that only the teacher's language needs to appear here. Note the constant support offered to the learner through the reinforcement of each stage of the process of language manipulation:

> *Qu'est-ce que c'est en français* 'I did not watch TV'*?*

> *Alors, qu'est-ce que c'est en français* 'I do not have'*?*

> *Tu as oublié?* 'I do not have' *en français* [points to two adjacent posters, including pages 58–59], *c'est le numéro cinq ou le numéro six?*

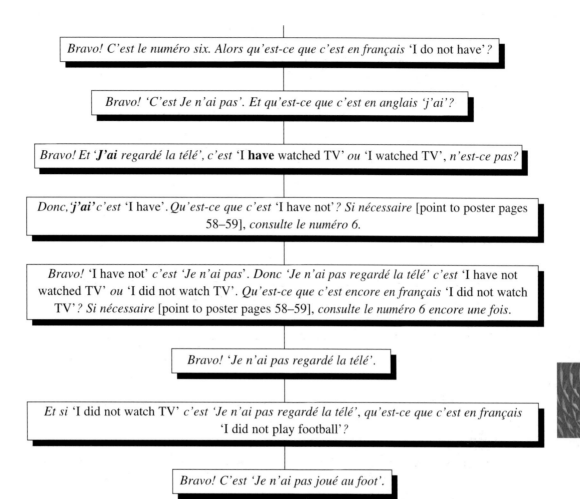

> *Bravo! C'est le numéro six. Alors qu'est-ce que c'est en français 'I do not have'?*

> *Bravo! 'C'est Je n'ai pas'. Et qu'est-ce que c'est en anglais 'j'ai'?*

> *Bravo! Et '**J'ai** regardé la télé', c'est 'I **have** watched TV' ou 'I watched TV', n'est-ce pas?*

> *Donc, 'j'ai' c'est 'I have'. Qu'est-ce que c'est 'I have not'? Si nécessaire* [point to poster pages 58–59], *consulte le numéro 6.*

> *Bravo! 'I have not' c'est 'Je n'ai pas'. Donc 'Je n'ai pas regardé la télé' c'est 'I have not watched TV' ou 'I did not watch TV'. Qu'est-ce que c'est encore en français 'I did not watch TV'? Si nécessaire* [point to poster pages 58–59], *consulte le numéro 6 encore une fois.*

> *Bravo! 'Je n'ai pas regardé la télé'.*

> *Et si 'I did not watch TV' c'est 'Je n'ai pas regardé la télé', qu'est-ce que c'est en français 'I did not play football'?*

> *Bravo! C'est 'Je n'ai pas joué au foot'.*

While some learners will commit to memory immediately that *'je n'ai pas'* is how to begin negative statements with *avoir* verbs in the *passé composé*, many will need future re-enactments of the scene above. These re-enactments will gradually get shorter until you can refer to a poster as an *aide-mémoire*:

L: *Qu'est-ce que c'est en français 'I have not done my homework'?*

T: [points to poster pages 58–59] *Le numéro 6.*

L: *Je n'ai pas …* (hesitates as to how to continue)

T: *Bravo! Qu'est-ce que c'est en français 'I **did** my homework'?*

L: *J'ai fait mes devoirs.*

T: *Bravo! Et 'J'ai fait mes devoirs' c'est 'I **did** my homework' et aussi 'I have done my homework'. Alors qu'est-ce que c'est en français 'I have not done my homework'?*

L: *Je n'ai pas fait mes devoirs.*

T: *Bravo!*

The list of classroom target language expressions overleaf shows which language points or structures each poster can serve to illustrate. The suggestions are not exhaustive. The aim is to show how lexical items with which learners are familiar can be used to demonstrate key aspects of French grammar at appropriate times. Whether and when you draw learners' attention to a particular point will depend on when the point best illustrates what learners need to know. For example, most pupils will be able to reproduce *'J'ai oublié mon cahier'* [photocopiable pages 64–65] long before you formally introduce the *passé composé*. As soon as you introduce the *passé composé* with *avoir*, however, directing learners to think about *'J'ai oublié mon cahier'* will help them visualise and retain the pattern.

Classroom target language expression on posters	Language points or structures it can serve to illustrate

Classroom target language expression on posters

> **Bonjour, ça va?**
>
> **Ça va bien merci.**
>
> **Au revoir.**

> **s'il te plaît**
> **s'il vous plaît**
>
> **excuse-moi**
> **excusez-moi**

> **Comment**
> **ça s'écrit?**
>
> A B E F I O Q
> H C   L J   U
> K D   M X

> G   N Y
> P   R
> T   S
> V   Z
> W

> **Qu'est-ce que**
> **c'est**
> **en français ...?**

Language points or structures it can serve to illustrate

Page 40

These expressions demonstrate how translating from one language into another does not necessarily involve word-for-word translations; and that, since each French expression here could be expressed in several ways in English, the key is to think about meaning when trying to say something in another language. You might wish to elaborate by pointing out that:

- *bonjour* literally means 'good day' and can translate 'hello', 'good morning' or 'good afternoon'
- *ça va?* literally means 'how is it going?', and therefore 'how are you?' and more familiar expressions like 'all right?'
- *merci* could be translated by 'thank you', 'thanks', 'cheers' and even 'ta'
- *revoir* in *au revoir* means 'to see again', as in 'Till we see each other again'; usually pronounced *auvoir*, showing how we frequently omit some sounds when uttering very common words

Page 41

- you address a young person, friend or relative differently from an older person who is not a relative

Pages 42–43

- if learners forget how to pronounce a particular letter, they can work it out by checking which sound column it is in, since all the letters in a column contain the same key sound. You can add accents to columns as they arise: *é* at the foot of the **B C D ...** column, for instance; and add *aide-mémoires* from learners' own experience, for example by writing *je* beside the letter **E**

Pages 44–45

- *Qu'est-ce que?* = what?
- 's' sound is the *ce*
- *ce que* and not *Qu'est-ce que* translates 'what' in expressions like *ce que je fais le week-end*

? ? ? ? ?

Comment ça s'écrit?

Je peux parler en anglais?

Je peux avoir

_____ **?**

Je suis en retard.

Pages 46–47

- *comment* = how
- use of third person reflexive to translate passive, as in '*Comment ça se prononce?*'

Pages 48–49

- there is no need to invert subject and verb in French questions
- *je peux* takes infinitive; many infinitives end in *-er*

Pages 50–51

- reinforces fact that *je peux* takes infintive [cf page 49, '*Je peux parler en anglais*']
- *-ir* is another infinitive ending

Note: the speech bubble is left empty and the line under the text left blank to show that anything can be requested using '*Je peux avoir…?*'. You may wish to make several photocopied versions of these two pages and insert illustrations and text for your pupils' most common requests, e.g. 'Can I have a merit?'

Pages 52–53

- *je suis* = I am
- *je* = I

chapter 4

23

Pages 54–55

- *je* becomes *j'* before a vowel
- difference in meaning between *je suis* and *j'étais*
- *être* and 'to be' are both irregular verbs which do not follow a pattern, unlike the three regular verbs of the five verbs on photocopiable pages 80 to 82

| J'étais avec | Monsieur _____ . |
| | Madame _____ . |

Pages 56–57

- *il* = he
- *elle* = she
- adjectives agree with the subject
- useful language when exploiting: '"*il*", *c'est masculin ou féminin?*'

| Il | est | absent. |
| Elle | | absente. |

Pages 58–59

- *n' ... pas* here conveys 'not'
- *je n'ai pas de* different from *je n'aime pas* [page 71]
- to say 'I do not have a ...' in French, 'a' replaced by *de*

Je n'ai pas de	livre.
	stylo.
	partenaire.

Pages 60–61

- reinforces fact that *je peux* takes infinitive
- *un* and *une* = 'a'
- to remember *avoir* = to have, think of *avoir*

| Je peux avoir | un livre? |
| | une feuille? |

up, up and away!

24

**C'est
quelle
page?**

J'ai oublié | mon cahier.

ma feuille.

mes devoirs.

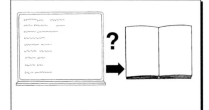

**On copie
ça?**

Tu aimes ...?

Pages 62–63

- *quel, quelle, quels, quelles* translate 'what something' [cf page 45, where *qu'est-ce que?* translates 'what?' on its own, hence *c'est quelle page? quelle heure? quelle sorte de?* and by extension, *quel bus?, quel quai?*
- you can show that no French word sounds exactly like an English word, even if spelt the same, by getting learners to repeat the French word *page* and compare it with the sound of the English word 'page'

Pages 64–65

- there are three words for 'my' – *mon, ma, mes* – *j'ai oublié* translates literally 'I have forgotten' and will be a useful, familiar example of the *passé composé* when you introduce this tense
- the *–é* ending on *oublié* and the *–er* of *cahier* sound the same, and contain the same sound as the letter column **B C D ...** on photocopiable pages 42–43

Pages 66–67

- *on* conveys idea of 'we'
- 'do' in English question forms, as in 'do we copy that?', is not translated in French
- unless accented as in *oublié* on pages 64–65, a final *–e* in French is not normally pronounced, as in *copie*

Pages 68–69

- unless accented, the final letter of a French word is not normally pronounced
- verb endings change in French (pages 70–71, *j'aime* but this page *tu aimes*) just as they do in English ('I like', 'she likes') although they change more in French
- 'do' in English question forms, as in 'do you like ...?' is not translated in French

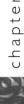

J'aime. | Je n'aime pas.

Pages 70–71

- both *j'* and *je* mean 'I', with *je* becoming *j'* before a vowel sound. You can demonstrate how the apostrophe shows that you have removed a letter – here, the *e* in *je* – by asking learners to explain what missing letters are represented by apostrophes in common English words like 'don't' and 'he's'
- to remind learners that *j'aime* and *j'ai* mean completely different things, point out that the *m* sound in *j'aime* is like the 'mmm' we say if we like something

Je pense que ...

Pages 72–73

- *que* after a verb usually means 'that'

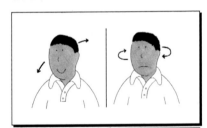

Je suis d'accord. | Je ne suis pas d'accord.

Pages 74–75

- *ne ... pas* conveys the idea of 'not' and goes around the verb
- *d'accord* means 'in agreement', so *je suis* and *je ne suis pas* mean 'I am' and 'I am not'

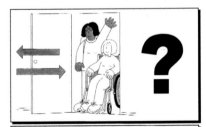

On peut | entrer?

sortir?

Pages 76–77

- to change a question from 'Can I ...?' to 'Can we ...?', change '*Je peux ... ?*' to *On peut ...?*
- as with *je peux*, *on peut* takes an infinitve

**Vous
pouvez
m'aider?**

PASSÉ

j'ai joué
j'ai regardé
j'ai écouté
j'ai fait
je suis | allé
| allée

PRÉSENT

je joue
je regarde
 j'écoute
je fais
je vais

FUTUR

je vais jouer
je vais regarder
je vais écouter
je vais faire
je vais aller

Pages 78–79

■ verbs change, and *je peux, on peut* and *vous pouvez* are all parts of the same verb
■ almost all irregular verbs in the present tense of the *vous* form end in *–ez*

Pages 80–82

Displaying these posters side by side as a timeline, with the *passé* to the left and the *futur* to the right of the *présent*, you can reinforce the verb patterns determined by each tense as well as encouraging correct pronunciation, for example, by asking learners to listen to the sounds at the end of the verbs:

T: *Au présent, on prononce le –e, oui ou non?* (Point to each final –e as you say it.) *Je joue, je regarde, j'écoute.*

Class: *Non.*

T: *Bravo! Alors prononcez en français* 'I play, I am playing'.

Class: *Je joue.*

T: *Bravo! Et prononcez en français* 'I watch, I am watching'.

Class: *Je regarde.*

You can also demonstrate:

■ how the *–é* ending in the *passé composé* sounds identical to the *–er* ending in the infinitives in the *futur* column;
■ how the first person of the *passé composé* must begin with either *j'ai* or *je suis*, but most of the time with *j'ai;*
■ that only past participles after *je suis* (and therefore after *être* verbs, agree with the subject, as in *je suis allé/allée*)
■ how you must include *je vais* plus an infinitve in the simple future, with *je vais* translating 'I am going', and the *–er* and *–re* endings in the infinitves on poster 82 translating 'to' (as in 'I am going to play/to watch/to listen, etc.)

There are tips on further exploiting photocopiable pages 80 to 82 [the three verb posters] in Chapter 5, (Building a verb wall).

Chapter **5**

Creating your own departmental posters

School specials

Each school has its own routines, hence the importance of adapting photocopiable pages 50–51 (*Je peux avoir…?*) to suit your own school's reward system. Some of my own 'school specials' include:

■ *Je rendais le registre;*

■ *Je rangeais les chaises* (in the hall after assembly).

Each new phrase will help highlight key points of grammar which learners can use to extend their own target language proficiency. The two phrases above are clearly very useful models when introducing the imperfect tense.

Like many schools, we also have our fair share of pupils who need to say:

'*Je suis sous observation*' ('I am on report'). When trying to find the target language for aspects of our own school's routines which might be unknown in French-speaking schools, ask native speakers to come up with the best equivalent term they can. If you do not have access to native speakers, create your own version. (You can start by creating your own version of the subject PSHE – Personal, Social and Health Education – into French!)

Further classroom target language expressions

The list below gives pupil expressions which typically follow on from those on the posters in this ResourceFile.

Je peux | *distribuer les cahiers?*
| *les livres?*
| *les feuilles?*

Je peux effacer le tableau?

Quelle est la date aujourd'hui?

J'ai fini.

Je n'ai pas fini.

Qu'est-ce que je fais?

Qu'est-ce qu'on fait?

Je peux travailler avec …?

Je peux | *ouvrir* | *la fenêtre?*
| *fermer* |

Je ne vois pas bien.

Tu as eu quelle note?
J'ai eu neuf sur dix.

Tu m'énerves!
Il | *m'énerve!*
Elle |

Have text, what next?

If you have access to a wordprocessor, experiment with font styles and sizes on computer. Always type in the longest line of text first to gauge what will fit, and if in doubt, print off a page of rough text and place it on the wall to see if it can easily be read from all parts of the room. There is a temptation to fit as much text as possible onto a poster, but this is counter-productive if it makes the text too small to read easily from a distance.

Choose a font where all letters are crystal clear, and make the font 'bold' so it is easy to read. If you do not have access to a computer, use a thick black felt for the text. (The posters in this ResourceFile all started out handwritten.) If you or a colleague are artistic, make an illustration for the poster which you can then combine with the text. You may even be able to find an artistic pupil willing to do the artwork. However, if like me, you cannot draw to save your life, remember that there is less need for artwork now. Since learners' linguistic competence will have developed significantly through planned use of the posters, they will not need the same level of visual support as they did at first. So you could:

■ include posters of text only;

■ include posters of French text beside the corresponding English text.

Building a verb wall

'Learners of all abilities are much more likely to grasp and work with grammatical structures if these are presented not through formal exposition but through demonstrations which make a strong visual or aural impression and require an active response.'

National Curriculum Final Report, Chapter 9: 'Sounds Words and Structures'

While posters of complete paradigms of verbs in different tenses can be very useful, many pupils need to arrive at an understanding of a verb paradigm in a carefully structured way. **Photocopiable pages 80–82** [verbs in three tenses] are an important first step in this direction. By displaying these posters as a timeline, with the past to the left and the future to the right of the present, you are offering learners a concrete means of getting to grips with the concept of tenses. However, this concept can be expanded enormously, as shown by the examples below. These examples are from the Key Stage 3 French course, *Génial 3* (reprinted by permission of Oxford University Press).

The table below focuses on the first person of verbs most commonly used by our pupils. The timeline sequencing of the three tenses reinforces the differences between each tense, while the highlighting of certain parts of each verb highlights the pattern. The questions at the foot of the page encourage simple conversation in different tenses.

The final column – and the arrows which direct the eye to it – encourages learners to create meaningful sentences from each verb. So a learner who needs to say 'I listened to music':

■ locates *de la musique* in the end column;

■ finds the correct tense column for 'I listened to';

■ goes down the *passé* column to the line which has *de la musique* at the very end;

■ links the two parts of the phrase, *j'ai écouté* and *de la musique*.

Les verbes 1

1. Lis

	PASSÉ	PRÉSENT	FUTUR	
to play	*I played* *I have played*	*I play* *I am playing*	*I am going to play*	
jou**er**	J'ai jou**é**	je jou**e**	je **vais** jou**er**	au tennis
regard**er** *to watch*	J'ai regard**é**	je regard**e**	je **vais** regard**er**	la télé
écout**er** *to listen*	J'ai écout**é**	j'écout**e**	je **vais** écout**er**	de la musique
achet**er** *to buy*	J'ai achet**é**	j'ach**è**t**e**	je **vais** achet**er**	des vêtements
fai**re** *to do*	J'ai fai**t**	je fai**s**	je **vais** fai**re**	du vélo
all**er** *to go*	Je suis all**é** Je suis all**ée**	je vai**s**	je **vais** all**er**	au cinéma
rest**er** *to stay*	Je suis rest**é** Je suis rest**ée**	je rest**e**	je **vais** rest**er**	à la maison

2. Travail à deux

Qu'est-ce que tu as fait hier?	Qu'est-ce que tu fais le week-end?	Qu'est-ce que tu vas faire demain?
What did you do yesterday?	*What do you do at the weekend?*	*What are you going to do tomorrow?*

Source: From *Génial 3* (Oxford University Press)

You could create your own verb wall using the layout shown in the two tables as a guide, with each verb, for example, on its own A4 sheet. You can further reinforce the difference between each tense by:

■ using paper of a different colour for each tense;

■ using boxes and bold text to highlight the key parts of each verb which characterise its tense.

The table below is for learners who are ready to work with complete paradigms of verbs. As well as including all parts of each verb, the final column allows learners to use each verb in a variety of meaningful sentences.

Les verbes 2

1. Lis

	PASSÉ	PRÉSENT	FUTUR	
	Hier… La semaine dernière…	Aujourd'hui … Normalement …	Demain La semaine prochaine …	
jou**er** *to play*	j'ai tu as il a elle a **joué** nous avons vous avez ils ont elles ont	je joue tu jou**es** il joue elle joue nous jou**ons** vous jou**ez** ils jou**ent** elles jou**ent**	je **vais** tu vas il va elle va **jouer** nous allons vous allez ils vont elles vont	au basket au tennis aux jeux vidéo du piano
regard**er** *to watch*	j'ai tu as il a elle a **regardé** nous avons vous avez ils ont elles ont	je regarde tu regard**es** il regarde elle regard**e** nous regard**ons** vous regard**ez** ils regard**ent** elles regard**ent**	je **vais** tu vas il va elle va **regarder** nous allons vous allez ils vont elles vont	la télé des vidéos un match de football un feuilleton
écout**er** *to listen*	j'ai tu as il a elle a **écouté** nous avons vous avez ils ont elles ont	j'écoute tu écout**es** il écoute elle écoute nous écout**ons** vous ecout**ez** ils écout**ent** elles écout**ent**	je **vais** tu vas il va elle va **écouter** nous allons vous allez ils vont elles vont	de la musique la radio des cassettes des C.D.
2. Travail à deux	Qu'est-ce que tu as fait hier? Qu'est-ce que tu as fait la semaine dernière?	Qu'est-ce que tu fais aujourd'hui? Qu'est-ce que tu fais le week-end?	Qu'est-ce que tu vas faire demain? Qu'est-ce que tu vas faire la semaine prochaine?	

Source: From *Génial 3* (Oxford University Press)

As well as supporting your teaching of the manipulation of verbs – the key area for pupil progression – a verb wall enables learners to expand their responses to the three most important questions for demonstrating achievement at level 6 of the revised National Curriculum and achieving a high grade in languages exams at 16+:

■ What did you do?

■ What do you do?

■ What are you going to do?

Whether asked in the context of conversation topics such as school, holidays or free time, it is these three questions more than any others which allow pupils to demonstrate the ability to discuss past, present and future events.

Once learners can say two things they did last night, they should try and say four things they did last night. Once they can say four, they should go for eight. You will need to remind them to use conjunctions and other link words to extend their utterances:

'J'ai fait mes devoirs **puis** j'ai regardé la télé.'

'Je suis allé au parc **où** j'ai joué au foot.'

Creating key word and key phrase posters

You can do this by displaying key word and key phrase lists, and referring learners to these whenever they need to extend their utterances. The other essential requirement for demonstrating achievement at level 6 of the revised National Curriculum and achieving a high grade in languages exams at 16+ is the expression of opinions. Photocopiable pages 70–75 [*j'aime, je pense que, je suis d'accord*, etc.] help learners express opinions in the present tense, but you can also show them how to form opinions in other tenses with another simple timeline of three posters:

| **passé** | **présent** | **futur** |
| c'était super | c'est super | ça va être super |

The selection of help boxes below is reproduced from the pupil's books and workbooks of *Génial 1, 2* and *3*. The boxes are designed to:

■ encourage learners to extend utterances by showing how known language can be put together to create more interesting language;

■ reinforce key link words;

■ reinforce the meaning of key words within structures.

Examples of help boxes from the *Génial* Key Stage 3 course (Oxford University Press)

Très utile

qui	who
aussi	also
mais	but
et	and

Je m'appelle Paul **et** j'ai quinze ans.
J'ai une sœur **qui** s'appelle Anne.
J'ai **aussi** un frère, Luc.
J'ai un chien, **mais** je n'ai pas de chat.

par contre	on the other hand
surtout	especially
ne ... pas	not
n' ... pas	not

Très utile

J'adore le poisson. **Par contre**, je n'aime pas le poulet.

J'aime le fast-food, **surtout** les hamburgers.

Je **ne** vais **pas** aller au McDo ce soir.

Très utile

l'année dernière	last year
je suis allé/allée	I went
je vais	I go

L'année dernière je suis allé en France, mais normalement **je vais** en Espagne pendant les grandes vacances.

		a	the	to the at the	some	my
AU SINGULIER	MASCULIN	un	le	au	du	mon
	FÉMININ	une	la	à la	de la	ma
before a vowel		–	l'	à l'	de l'	mon
AU PLURIEL		–	les	aux	des	mes

When creating posters along these lines for your own pupils, always begin by asking what expressions learners need most. If you have access to a colour printer, you can use coloured print for link words in the middle of sentences, which is how they are highlighted in the *Génial* pupil's books. Otherwise, you can box or underline the link words.

Creating opportunities

Learners need lots of opportunities to practise and reinforce language they have learned. One way of getting them to practise conversing in one or more tenses is to write on the OHP one or more questions before pupils enter the room:

Pupils begin the lesson by asking and answering the questions in pairs. You can refer them to the verb posters and link word posters to get them started or, for learners who need more support, write up a limited range of answers on the OHP. This is, of course, the perfect context for questions like '*Qu'est-ce que c'est en français,* "I didn't do anything last night."*?*'

As with all aspects of language teaching, it is better to set a task learners can practise well than one they will do badly if at all. You may well need to start with one question on the OHP when pupils come in, then in later lessons increase this to two questions in the same tense:

■ *Qu'est-ce que tu as fait hier soir?*

■ *Qu'est-ce que tu as fait après?*

When learners are ready to switch tense, start by getting them to switch between two. Obviously when they are comfortable with switching between two tenses you can move them onto three.

Alternatively, for a quieter start to the lesson, you can get learners to practise writing answers to the questions on the OHP.

Chapter **6**

Developing your department's target language policy

'Departments should agree on a policy for consolidating or extending the use of the target language by teacher and pupils, to ensure that the target language is used consistently by all members of the department with shared expectations of pupils' use of it.'
MFL non-statutory guidance

35

It took several years to develop fully the materials and methodology in this ResourceFile. While introducing both from scratch to any department is a major task, the pay-off can be enormous over time, in terms of the increase in learners' ability to:

■ develop their listening skills, pronunciation and intonation;

■ understand key structures;

■ manipulate target language;

■ extend their target language;

■ better equip themselves for further study.

In drawing up a policy on increasing pupil target language use you will need to set manageable goals. You may wish to consider doing any of the following:

■ arranging to visit any modern languages departments in your area which you believe are using good practice in encouraging pupil target language use (this is easier if your authority has an MFL adviser who can direct you);

■ drawing up a departmental minimum list of words and phrases for each year group.

You can adhere closely to the suggested order of introduction of expressions in this ResourceFile, or adapt it to suit the particular needs of your own pupils. Overleaf is a list of words and phrases for Key Stage 3, drawn up by one department.

Lists of words and phrases for Key Stage 3 drawn up by one department

First term essentials	Objective:	to ensure that every pupil has a basic stock of language in order to operate within the target language.
	To be learnt:	basic classroom objects; understanding and giving simple instructions; how to say 'yes/no'; how to ask politely for things; how to say thank you/please; how to say 'I don't know/don't understand'; how to spell and ask for words to be spelt; how to give a simple opinion; how to say 'I've finished'; how to ask for meaning and clarification; how to ask permission to do something.
By the end of Year 7	Objective:	to extend pupils' stock of classroom and organisational phrases.
	To be learnt:	how to offer something; how to give, as well as understand, more complex instructions; how to express agreement and disagreement; how to apologise; how to say 'perhaps'; how to express an opinion, with simple reasons; how to check whether something is OK or has been understood.
During Key Stage 3	Objective:	to enable pupils to express themselves, within the context of classroom business, as appropriate to individual pupils' progression.
	To be learnt:	how to offer to do something; how to ask what should be done (next); how to invite opinion; how to give a reason 'why'.

Source: National Curriculum Council, *Target Practice. Developing pupils' use of the target language*

Other things you may wish to consider when drawing up a departmental policy:

- Agreeing who will photocopy which posters and when.

- Deciding whether your posters will be coloured in and, if so, how, when, and by whom.

- Agreeing who will display the copies and where.

- Agreeing a system of praise and reward for pupil effort in using classroom target language.

- Discussing how you can encourage pupils to use and sustain the target language when working in pairs and groups.

- Recording (or, if you have a Foreign Language Assistant, asking him or her to record) the list of words and phrases onto cassette for pupil copying.

- Including in schemes of work at what point pupils should tackle the reinforcement activity sheets on pages 87 to 89.

up, up and away!

36

- Including in schemes of work how you will assess learners' proficiency in using the classroom expressions (please see pages 13–14 for more ideas).

- Deciding where pupils will note useful new classroom language words and phrases for quick reference (cover of exercise book? separate section in vocabulary book?).

- Making a cassette recording of your own lesson or lessons to help you evaluate your own development.

- Inviting colleagues to observe your own lessons and vice-versa, with each observer highlighting **all** the positive aspects and suggesting a **maximum** of two specific ways of further increasing pupil target language use.

- Agreeing when you will review how the policy is working.

- Discussing how your basic list of expressions might be extended later.

- Letting pupils, parents, colleagues in other departments and your school management know what you are doing and why it so important for learners.

- Discussing whether you can encourage pupils to set themselves targets in the target language.

- Always addressing all visitors to your classroom in the target language, and expecting them to respond back in the target language.

- If your department teaches more than one language, deciding how you will ensure consistency across different languages.

- Planning a departmental treat for all the hard work that has gone into implementing your pupil target language policy!

So, to conclude …

What am I aiming to change?	Next lesson	Next term	Next year
In myself			
With my colleagues			
With my learners			

Bon courage!

Section 2

Classroom language posters

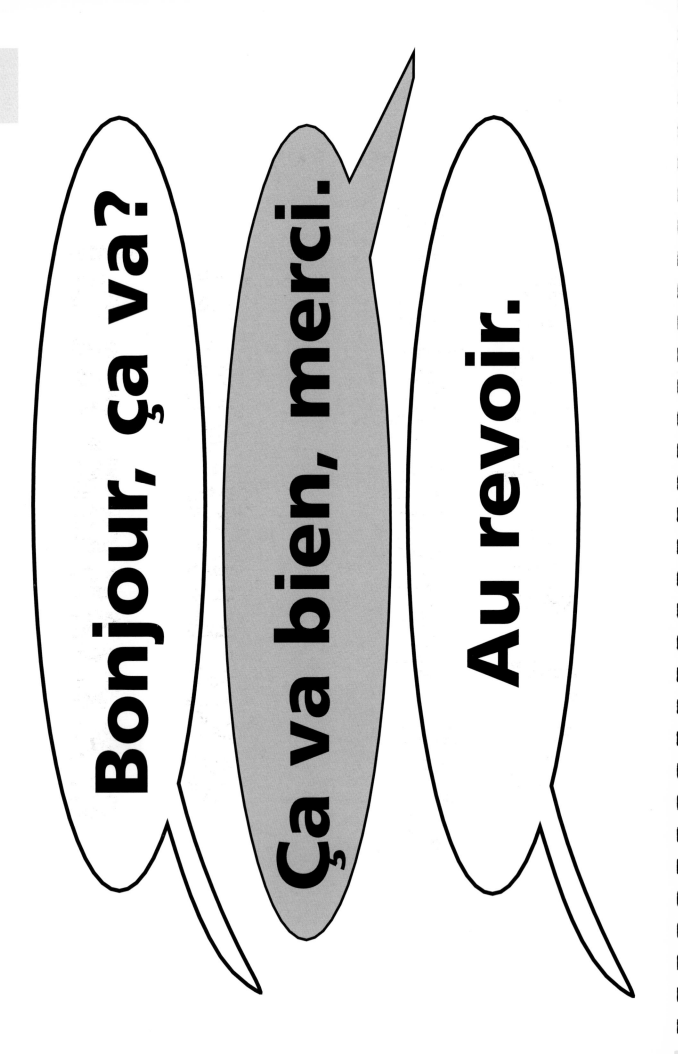

Bonjour, ça va?

Ça va bien, merci.

Au revoir.

s'il te plaît

s'il vous plaît

excuse-moi

excusez-moi

Comment ça s'écrit?

A B E F I O Q
H C L J O U
K D M X

G N Y

P R

T S Z

V

W

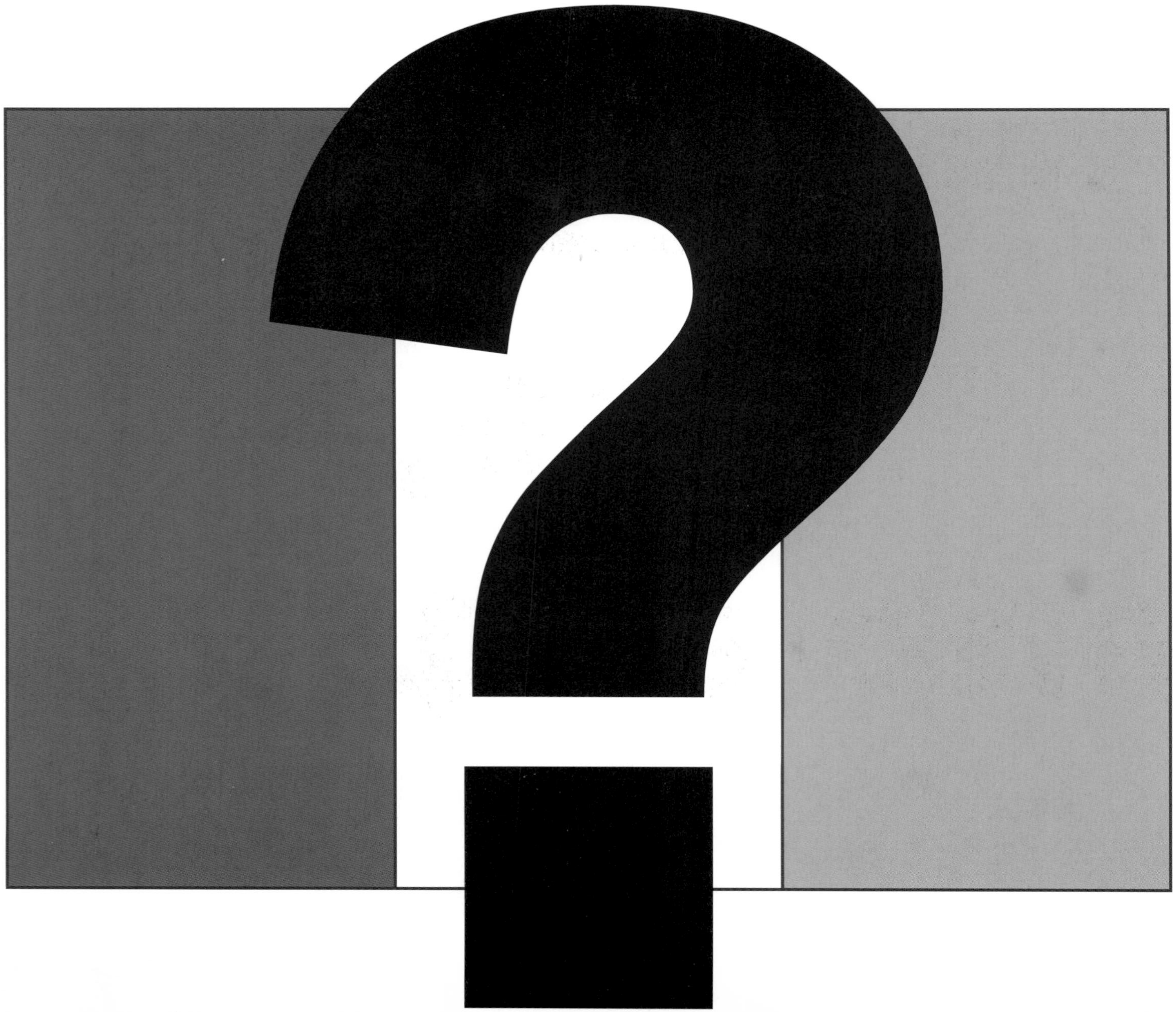

Qu'est-ce que c'est

c'est

en français ... ?

45

Comment ça s'écrit?

Je peux parler en anglais?

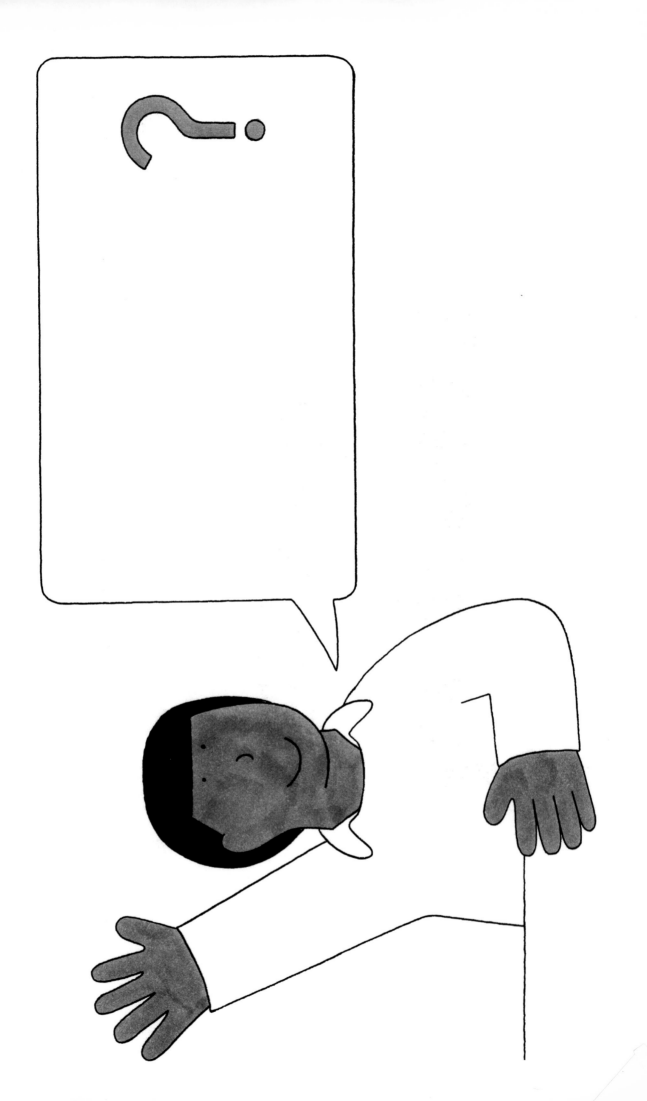

Je peux avoir ... ?

Je suis en retard.

J'étais avec

Monsieur ∎

Madame ∎

Il est absent.

Elle est absente.

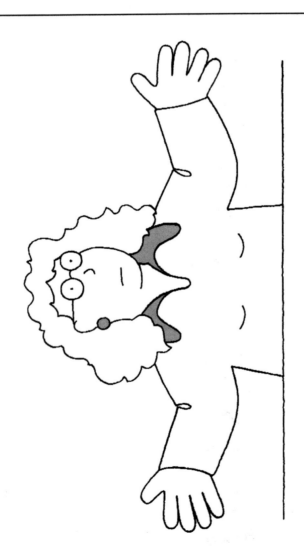

Je n'ai pas de livre.
stylo.
partenaire.

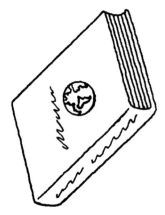

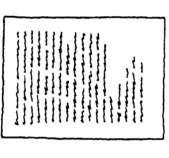

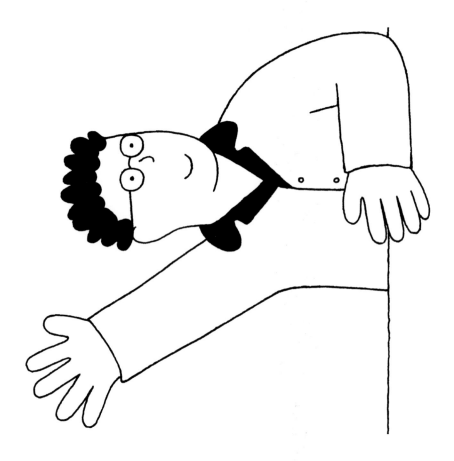

Je peux avoir | un livre
une feuille?

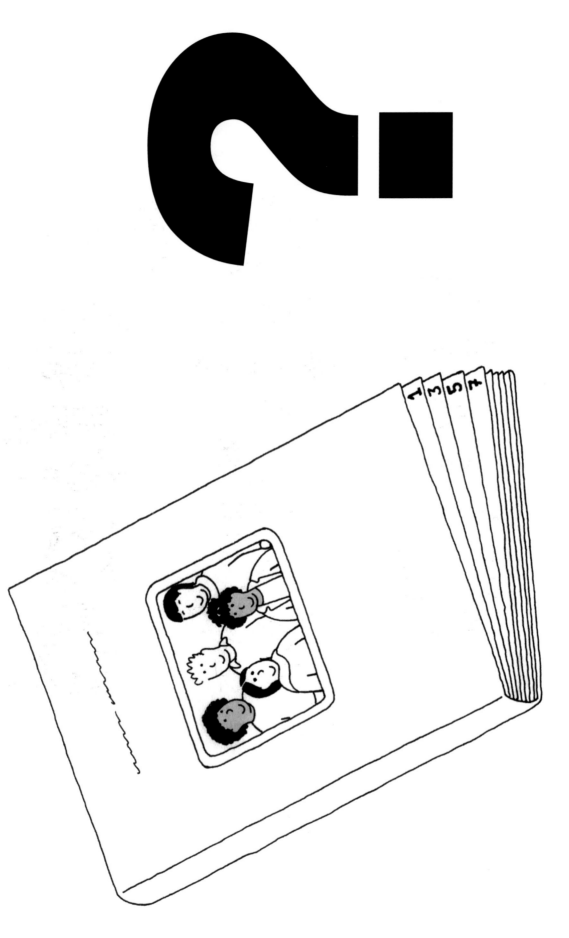

C'est quelle page ?

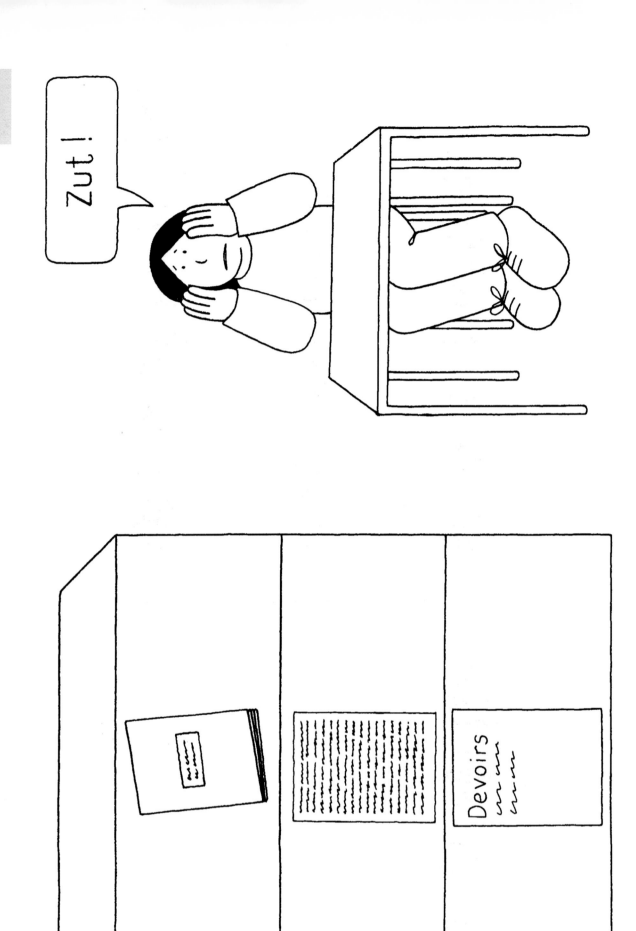

J'ai oublié

mon cahier.

ma feuille.

mes devoirs.

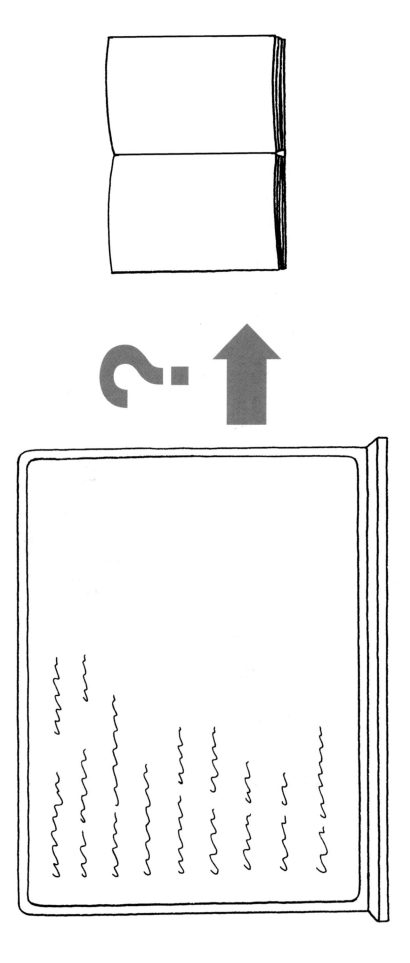

On copie ça?

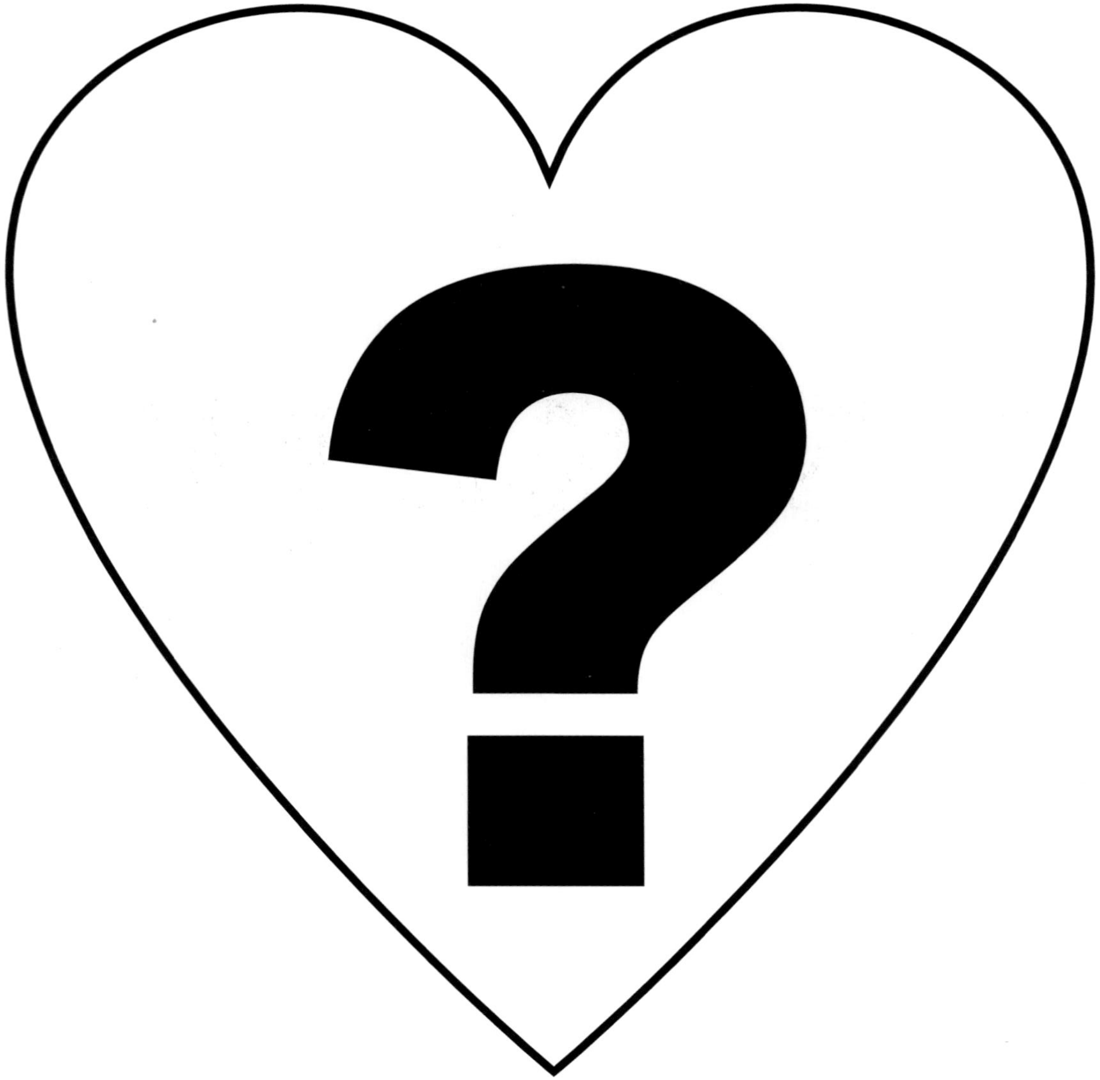

Tu aimes ... ?

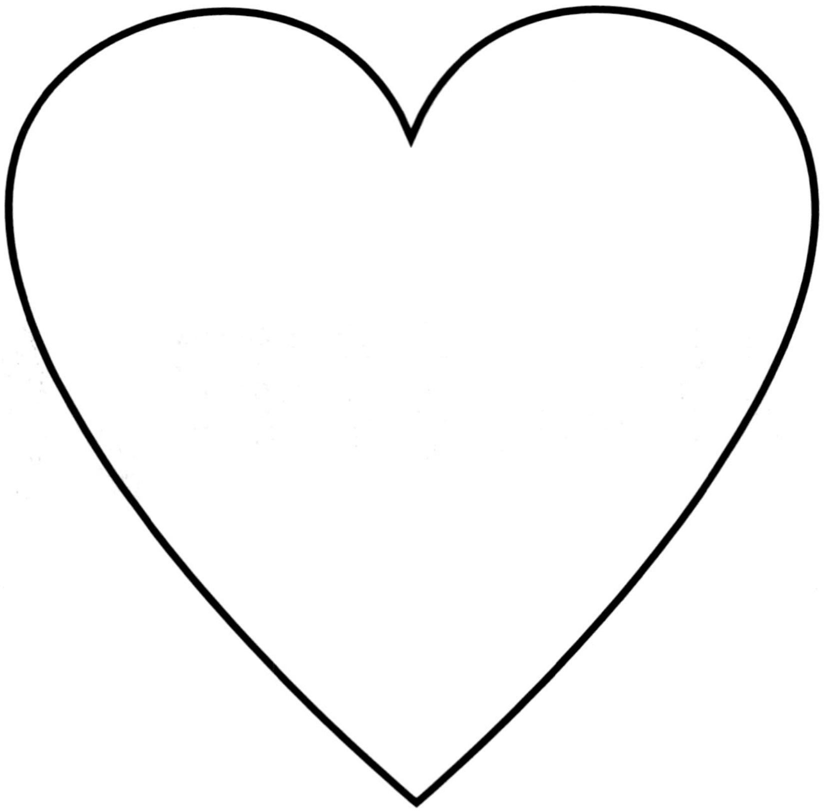

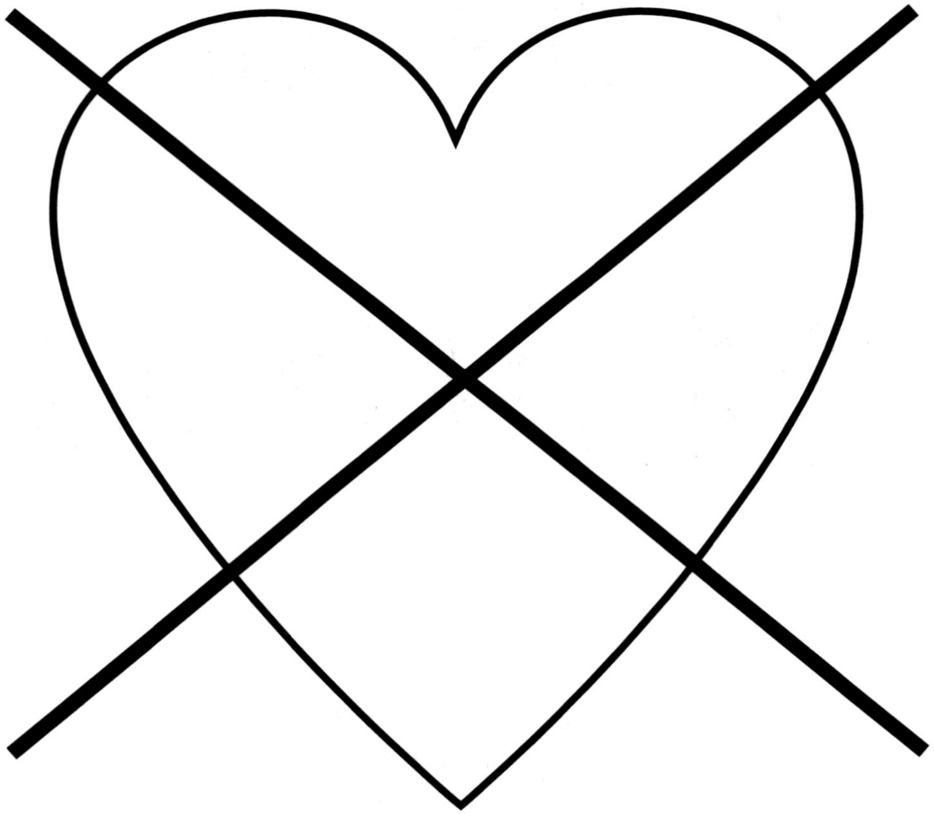

Je

n'aime

pas.

J'aime.

Je pense que ...

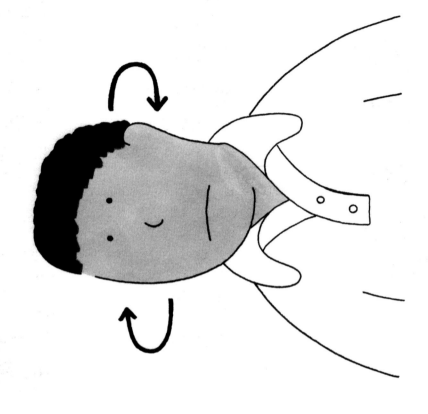

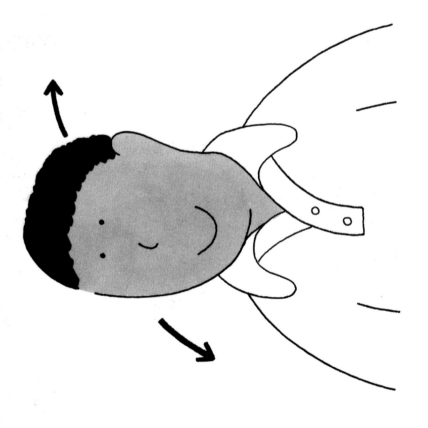

Je ne suis pas d'accord.

Je suis d'accord.

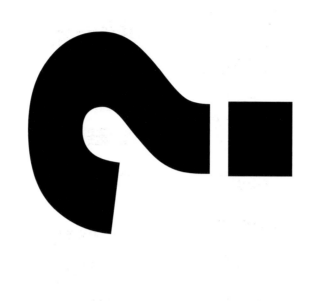

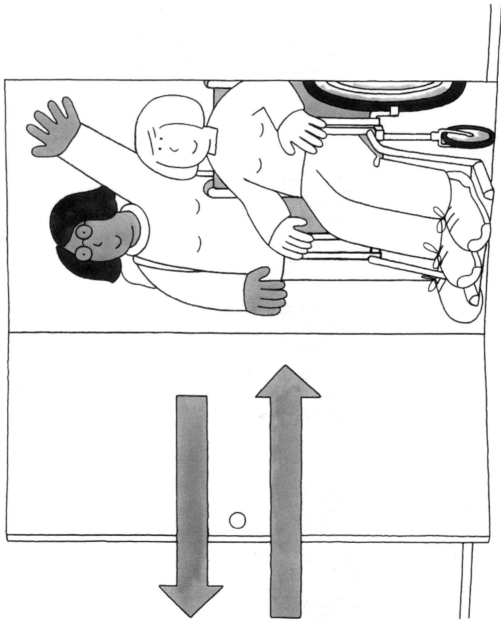

On peut entrer? sortir?

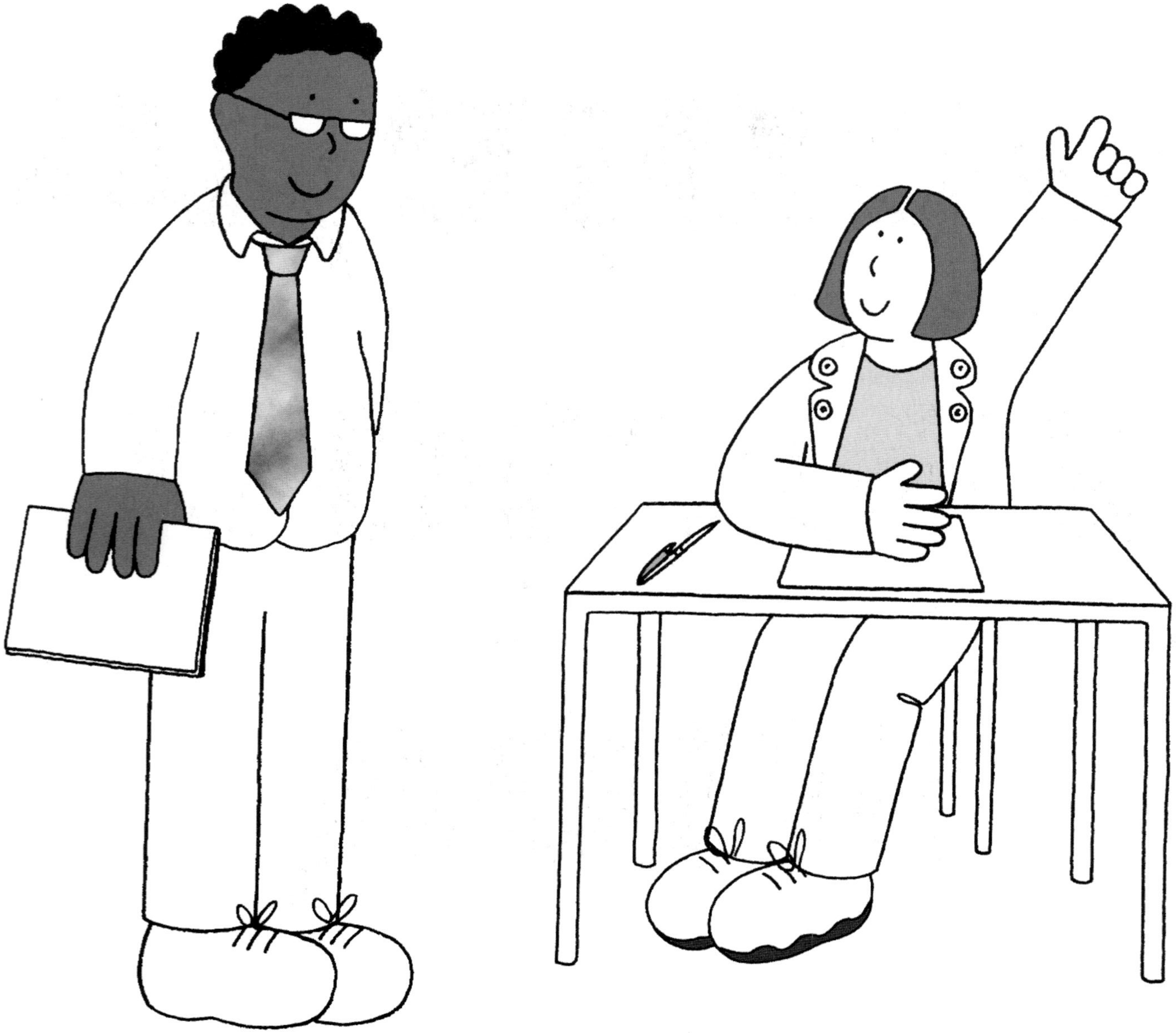

Vous pouvez m'aider?

PASSÉ

j'ai joué

j'ai regardé

j'ai écouté

j'ai fait

je suis | allé

allée

PRÉSENT

je joue

je regarde

j'écoute

je fais

je vais

FUTUR

je vais jouer

je vais regarder

je vais écouter

je vais faire

je vais aller

Section 3

Feuilles d'étudiant
&
Feuilles de consolidation

84

Bonjour, ça va? Ça va bien, merci. Au revoir.	**Hello, how is it going?** **It is going well, thanks.** **Goodbye.**
s'il te plaît **s'il vous plaît** **excuse-moi** **excusez-moi**	**please** **sorry**
?	**Qu'est-ce que** **c'est** **en français …?**
? ? ? ? ?	**Comment** **ça s'écrit?**
	**Je peux** **parler** **en anglais?**
	**Je peux** **avoir** **_____?**
	**Je suis** **en retard.**

Nom _____ classe _____

Feuille d'étudiant

	**J'étais avec** | **Monsieur** _____. | **Madame** _____.
	**Il** | **est** | **absent.** **Elle** | | **absente.**
	**Je n'ai pas de** | **livre.** **stylo.** **partenaire.**
	**Je peux avoir** | **un livre?** **une feuille?**
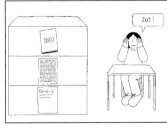	**C'est quelle page?**
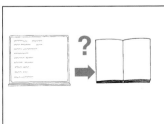	**J'ai oublié** | **mon cahier.** **ma feuille.** **mes devoirs.**
	On copie ça?

Nom _____ classe _____

Feuille d'étudiant

Tu aimes ...?

| J'aime. | Je n'aime pas. |

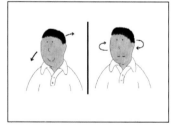

Je pense que ...

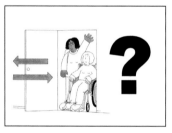

| Je suis d'accord. | Je ne suis pas d'accord. |

| On peut | entrer? sortir? |

Vous pouvez m'aider?

Mot mystère   Nom _____ classe _____

Complète et trouve le mot mystère.
Si necessaire, regarde la feuille 'En classe 1'.

		1	A	U		R	E	V	O	I	R					
				2							—					
3			'			—						'			
					4									
5													
			6		'									
	7												
	8											
9							'					

Clues

1. ⟨ Goodbye ⟩

2. ⟨ [Sorry] ⟩ (*said to a friend*).

3 **?** ____ ____ ____ en français?

4 **?** Qu'est-ce que c'est ____ ____ ?

5 Je peux parler ____ ____ ?

6 ⟨ Please ⟩ (*said to an adult who is not a friend or relative*)

7 ⟨ Can I have …? ⟩

8 ⟨ Hello, how is it going? ⟩

9 **? ? ? ? ?**

Feuille de consolidation B

Mot croisés Nom ______________________ classe ______

Complète.
Si nécessaire, regarde la feuille 'En classe 2'.

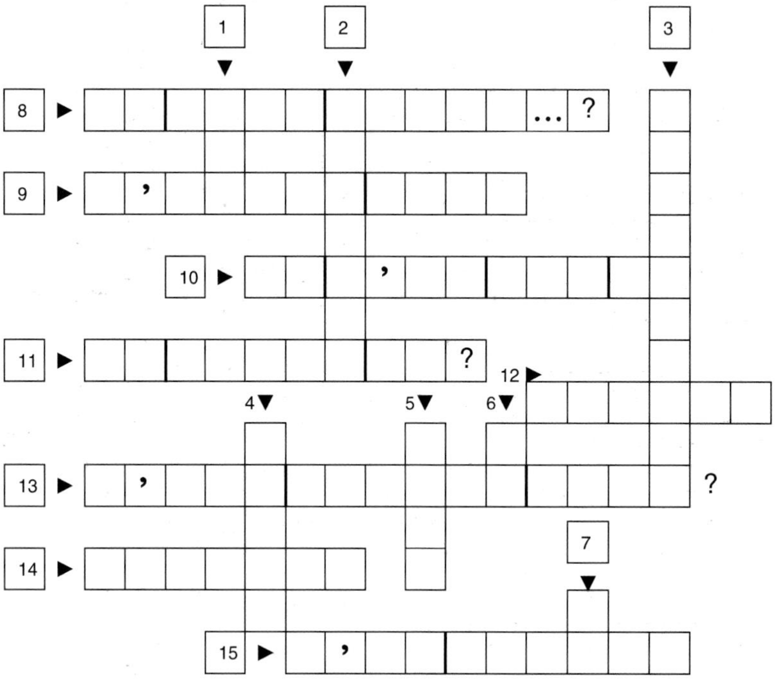

Clues

Verticalement

1 is __

2 absent (*féminin*) __

3 partner __

4 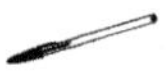 __

5 she __

6 I __

7 he __

Horizontalement

8 Can I have … ?

9 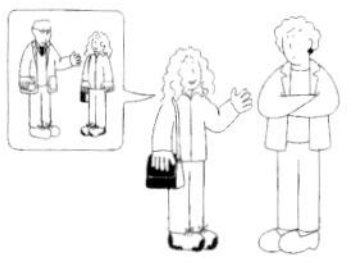 __ __ *Monsieur Brown*

10 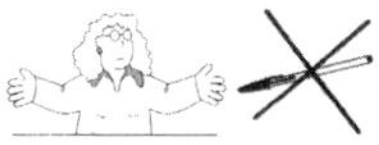 __ __ __ __ *stylo*

11 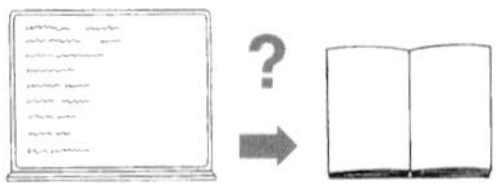

12 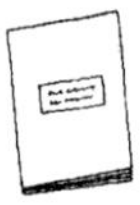

13 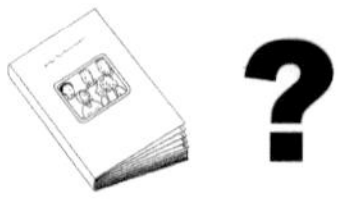

14 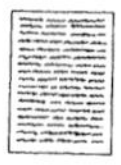

15 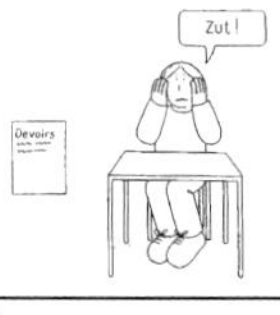

__ __ *mes devoirs*

Feuille de consolidation C

Trouve les mots   Nom _____ classe _____

Si nécessaire, regarde les feuilles 'En classe 1 à 7, 8 à 14 et 15 à 20.

J	E	N	E	S	U	I	S	P	A	S	B	T	V
F	L	J	E	P	E	U	X	A	V	O	I	R	G
G	L	E	N	A	N	G	L	A	I	S	C	R	F
J	E	P	E	U	X	P	A	R	L	E	R	D	X
J	E	S	U	I	S	E	N	R	E	T	A	R	D
O	N	P	E	U	T	E	N	T	R	E	R	C	L
J	E	S	U	I	S	D	'	A	C	C	O	R	D
H	K	V	O	U	S	P	O	U	V	E	Z	J	Q
D	J	'	É	T	A	I	S	J	'	A	I	M	E
E	J	S	T	Y	L	O	F	E	U	I	L	L	E
V	O	N	P	E	U	T	S	O	R	T	I	R	G
O	T	Q	E	R	C	O	M	M	E	N	T	F	R
I	J	E	N	'	A	I	M	E	P	A	S	Q	H
R	T	V	S	T	U	A	I	M	E	S	F	U	C
S	C	'	E	S	T	B	D	C	A	H	I	E	R

Clues

_ _ _ _ d'accord

je peux parler _ _ ?

_ _ _ en anglais?

_ quelle page?

je _ que

_ _ m'aider?

_ avec Madame Smith

_ ça s'écrit?

_ _ _ une feuille?

_ _ _ _

Can we come in? _ _ _ ?

Can we go out? _ _ _ _ ?

_

_ _ _

_ _ _

_ _ ?

un _

un _

une _

les _

he   _

she   _

Further reading (and viewing!)

Opening the door on the modern languages classroom
A video resource for INSET with supporting teacher's notes
University College of St Martin, Lancaster
(Teacher's Notes by James Burch) (CILT)

Target Practice. Developing pupils' use of the target language
Book and video
(National Curriculum Council)

Halliwell S and Jones B, *Teaching in the target language; Pathfinder 5* (CILT, 1991)

Holmes B, *Keeping on Target; Pathfinder 23* (CILT, 1994)

Elston T and McLagan P, *Génial parts 1, 2 and 3* (Oxford University Press)